THE WORLD FOLKTALE LIBRARY

Tales from Scandinavia

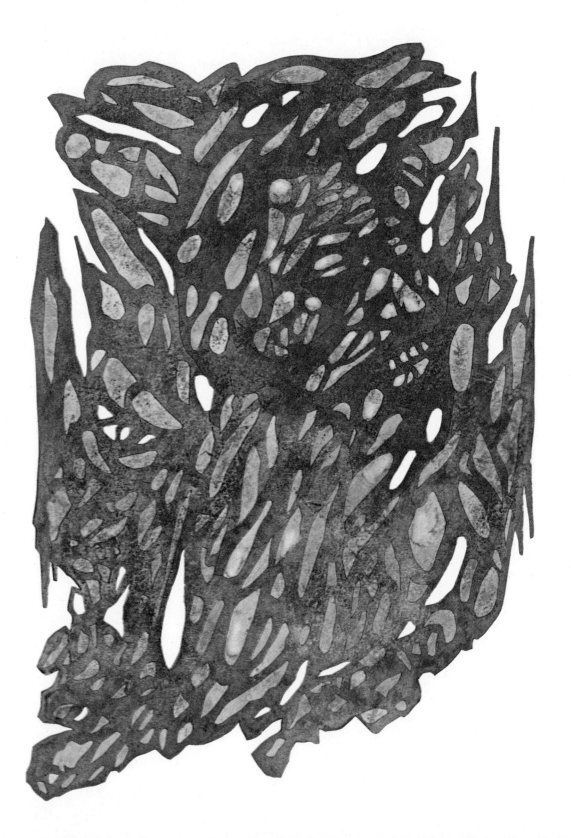

Tales from Scandinavia

By Frederick Laing

Illustrated by Leo and Diane Dillon

Consultants

Moritz A. Jagendorf
Author and Folklorist

Carolyn W. Field
Coordinator of Work with Children
The Free Library of Philadelphia

SILVER BURDETT COMPANY

Morristown, New Jersey
Glenview, Ill. • Palo Alto • Dallas • Atlanta

Library of Congress Catalog Card Number: 78-56060   ISBN 0-382-03355-8

INTRODUCTION

Folktales are not usually about real people or actual events, but in a way they are almost always true. They tell us something real about the people who pass them along and about where they live. Folktales often express the values of a society, or reveal that society's ideas about living and surviving. Sometimes the stories are about the joys and hopes of a people, as well as about their worries and fears. Each story tells us a little about life as certain people see it.

If you should find yourself among the people of the northern countries on a summer day, you might wonder if the sun ever sets and if night ever comes. Night does finally arrive, but lasts only for an hour or two. Then it's daylight again. That is why Scandinavia is known as the "Land of the Midnight Sun." Summer is lovely and magical, but its time is short. Winter is just the opposite. During the long winter, the people of these northern countries see the sun for only a brief time each day.

The early Scandinavians—who lived in Iceland, Norway, Sweden, and Denmark—looked upon winter as an enemy. It was hard to find food, keep warm, and even stay alive during the long, dark season. Scandinavian folktales tell of villains, who are usually giants, as big as icebergs and as cruel as the ice is cold. The heroes of these early Scandinavians were gods. They were as shining and warm as the summer sun, and could be as gentle as the mild summer days. There were many gods and giants, for it took many explanations and imaginary tales to explain the wonders of the world. In these ancient folktales, you will learn about how the gods and the giants were created, and how they in turn created the people.

THE EDITOR

*For Blanche
and her basket of golden apples*

CONTENTS

In the Beginning

In the beginning there was a vast, dark gap filled with ice and swirling fog. There were no gods, no giants or people; no animals, no birds or fish. There was no life of any kind. At the edge of this cold, dark space there was a steady, glowing fire.

Gradually the heat of the fire began to melt the ice. As it melted, a huge figure in the shape of a man was formed. He was called Ymir, and he was the first of the giants.

The ice continued to melt, forming a cow. Her name was Audhumbla, and she fed Ymir with her milk. Audhumbla had to eat, too, so she began to lick the ice. The ice was salty, but the cow liked the taste of salt. She licked and licked, until another form began to take shape.

On the first day Audhumbla uncovered hair, on the second day, a head, and by the third day, the rest of a beautiful new being. This time it was a god. His name was Buri, and he was the first of the gods.

One night, other young giants grew from Ymir's arm-
pit. That began the family of giants. From Buri, also,
children appeared. That was the start of the gods.

At first the gods tried to get along with the giants.
Buri's son married a giant's daughter. They had sons
who turned out to be gods like Buri. One of these was
Odin, who was born wise. He had a hunger for knowl-
edge. Because there was so much he wanted to know,
Odin, somehow, somewhere, traded one of his eyes for all
the wisdom of the world.

Odin knew the gods wanted to live in peace. They
wanted a world that would be bright and beautiful. He
knew the giants did not. He knew they hated the sun.
They wanted every place to be dark and cold. And they
really liked to cause trouble.

The gods increased in number and they grew in size.
And so did the giants. The first giant, Ymir, grew to be
the size of a mountain. The gods looked on and shook

their heads. If there were going to be so many trouble-some giants, and if they grew to be the size of Ymir, then the giants would have to be destroyed. All the gods agreed, including the wise Odin.

There was a battle between the gods and giants, and the frost giant, Ymir, was killed. A river of blood — cold as an arctic iceberg — poured from his deep wounds and covered the land. The other giants tried to escape, but they were drowned in Ymir's blood — all of them except Bergilmir and his wife, who had a boat and escaped to Jotunheim, a country at the edge of the world. They brought into being a new race of giants and prospered, for Jotunheim was the kind of dark and frosty region a giant liked best.

After the battle, the gods created a new world out of the mountainous corpse of Ymir. They made Midgard, or "middle garden," out of his flesh, and placed it in the middle of a vast space. Out of Ymir's sweat and blood, the

gods made the ocean, the rivers, and the lakes; and out of the giant's bones, the hills. His sharp teeth became the jagged cliffs, and his curly hair became the trees and the plants. His eyebrows were planted along the banks and the boundaries. When this was done, the gods raised his skull, like a massive dome, above the earth and sea to make the sky. And his brains became the shining clouds.

To support Ymir's skull, the gods found four strong dwarfs who lived deep in the underworld. The dwarfs stood at four points under the sky that once was Ymir's skull. Their names were Nordri, Sudri, Austri, and Westri, the four points of the compass.

Then the gods reached into the fire at the edge of space, drew out some embers, and threw them into the sky. The sparks became the stars. The two biggest embers became the sun and the moon. The sun brought light and warmth to the world and made the plants and trees grow.

When the giants saw the bright, new world the gods had created, they wanted to destroy it. They sent Skoll and Hati, their fiercest wolves, to chase after the sun and moon, and swallow them. But the gods made the sun and moon move faster than the wolves could run. This, the Norse people say, explains why the sun and moon move so swiftly across the northern sky.

One day the gods went to see how things were coming along in Midgard. The trees that sprang from Ymir's hair had grown and blossomed. The gods noticed two handsome trees near the bank of a river. They had grown so close that the leaves on their lower branches touched. The gods named the trees Ask and Embla.

Odin felt that the two beautiful trees should have something more than names, and because he was the god of wisdom, he gave them thought.

Then the gods gave Ask the form of a man, and Embla the form of a woman. Now Ask and Embla could walk. They could see and hear, and even smell the fragrance of a summer day. And they could think. But still there was something missing. They could not talk.

At last the gods gave them words, the power of speech. The first man and woman were complete, and they were the first of their kind to walk through the green forest of Midgard, the world of man.

That is the story the people in the north countries told of the creation of man, as they sat hugging their fires on the long, winter nights.

The Gold Necklace
and the Statue

The Norse gods lived in Asgard, a city high in the heavens. There were dazzling palaces with gold roofs, and the city was protected by high walls and towers. Odin, the leader of all the gods and the master of wisdom, was called the All-father. His throne was in the highest tower of the city of Asgard.

From his throne, Odin could see beyond Midgard, past the edge of the earth, and into the frosty shadows of Jotunheim. On each of his shoulders sat a big bird. Some say they were ravens. One was Hugin, who was Thought; the other was Munin, and he was Memory.

Each day the birds flew out from Asgard to the edge of darkness. Each evening they returned and told Odin what they had seen. Though the birds told Odin much about the world, there were things they did not tell the god about his own kingdom. They did not tell Odin about Frigga.

———◆———

Frigga was Odin's wife. She was a beautiful goddess, and spent a lot of time thinking of ways to make herself even more beautiful. Some of the gods thought she was more vain than wise.

In Asgard, there was a temple in honor of Odin. A gold statue of the god stood inside the temple. Something about the beautiful statue pleased and excited Frigga. She thought about the statue so much that she could hardly sleep.

One evening the goddess went to the temple to gaze with wonder at the statue of her husband. As she stood there, an idea struck her. When Frigga had an idea, it was usually a scheme to get a gem or a gown to set off her beauty.

"It's really a beautiful statue of Odin," she thought. "But what about me? After all, I am his wife. Why shouldn't I have a small part of this lovely statue?" And then a piece of the gold statue caught Frigga's eye. Some say it was the gold cord that tied Odin's robe.

"If I could break off that tiny piece," her thoughts ran on, "it could be made into a lovely necklace. A gold necklace would be very becoming to me. Odin's eyes will light up with admiration when he sees me wearing it! Who would miss such a tiny piece? Odin? No! He never

notices such little things." And she twisted off the piece of gold.

Frigga hurried back to the palace and gave the gold to her favorite servant. "Here, Fulla, take this to the dwarfs. Tell them to make me an ornament out of this piece of gold."

The dwarfs were unpleasant little creatures who lived in caves deep down under the earth. They often served the gods by making rare gifts for them in their forges. This time they made Frigga a beautiful necklace.

When Odin saw the necklace, his eyes did light up with admiration. "The gold matches the gleam in your hair," he said, never bothering to ask Frigga where she had got the necklace.

One day while Odin was in the temple, he suddenly noticed that something was wrong. A piece of the statue was missing! "What is the meaning of this? It's a sacrilege!" he roared.

He sent a messenger to the dwarfs. Odin suspected they would know something about the missing gold.

The next night two dwarfs came cringing to him. Odin pointed to the statue; his throat was so choked with anger that he could hardly speak. "Who?" he finally asked. "I order you to tell me! Who dared to steal a piece of this statue?"

The dwarfs could not answer. What could they say? Could they betray a goddess? No. Yet if they told Odin they knew nothing, he would probably find out that they were lying. They hung their heads and were silent.

Odin understood. "So it was one of the gods! I'll find out who it was," he told them. "I'll make this statue

talk, and I'll place it over the temple gates, where it can shout out the name of the thief."

When Frigga heard about Odin's plans, she trembled. She sent for Fulla. The good servant came at once to the goddess. "Go to the dwarfs and have them find a way to prevent the statue from talking," Frigga said.

"The dwarfs drive a hard bargain for favors," Fulla warned her.

"I know! But . . . . O Fulla, Odin must never find out. Never!" Frigga moaned, wringing her hands. "To think that just one little piece of gold could make him so furious!"

Fulla went to the underworld and told the dwarfs of Frigga's distress. At first they refused to help the goddess, for they were afraid of Odin. Finally one of the dwarfs said he would help the goddess, and he returned to the palace with Fulla. When Frigga saw the dwarf, she covered her eyes and screamed in horror. He was so ugly! Frigga had never before seen such a loathsome creature.

At last she uncovered her eyes. The dwarf merely grinned. He looked like a frog with long, yellow teeth. Frigga could hardly bear to look at him.

"If you wish to keep your secret from Odin," the dwarf said, grinning, "I'll see that the statue does not talk. But only on one condition."

"What is the condition?" Frigga asked nervously.

"I want you to smile at me. But wait, not an ordinary smile. You must smile as if you found me handsome, as if you loved me."

Frigga gasped. She forced the corners of her mouth upward, while her eyes stared at him in horror. The dwarf laughed out loud. The sound of his laughter was even worse than the sight of his face.

"No, no, my beautiful goddess," he said, wagging his stubby finger at her. "That will never do. For such a smile I would never stop the statue from telling everyone that you are the thief."

"Oh, please!" she begged, and again she forced a smile.

"You will have to do better than that. You must smile as if you found me more handsome than your husband," he insisted.

She kept trying to smile, though she hated the sight of the dwarf. At last the horrid creature was satisfied. He told Frigga he would have the statue broken into a thousand pieces. It would never talk, for it could never be put together again.

The ugly dwarf strutted away on his crooked little legs, chuckling to himself. He could hardly wait to tell the other dwarfs how he had humbled a goddess.

But the ugly dwarf kept his bargain. The statue was smashed into a thousand pieces. When Odin saw it, he was more than angry. He was insulted and deeply hurt. He believed his household, and perhaps even his kingdom, was against him. In silent fury, he left Asgard. He left his palace; he left his kingdom. He simply disappeared.

Frigga searched the palace and Asgard for Odin. She wanted to beg his forgiveness. She cried out his name. Then all the gods called to him. Then the men of Midgard called into the icy winds that swept the earth. "Odin! Odin!" they cried. But the god did not hear them. There was only silence.

Other gods tried to take Odin's place, but they failed. Dark days fell on the world and on the city of Asgard. Without Odin, the All-father, the skies became dark and cold winds swept over the city. The frost giants reached out their icy fingers. They nipped the buds, shriveled the leaves, froze the flowers, and killed the crops.

For seven long months Odin stayed away. Then he came back and forgave Frigga. When Odin saw the harm the frost giants had caused, he drove them back to Jotunheim, along with the howling, icy winds.

The sun came out again to warm the earth. The trees sprouted new buds, new crops grew, and bright flowers lifted their heads toward the fair skies.

Loki's Bet

Thor was the son of Odin, and the god of thunder. He had flaming-red hair and a fiery beard that gave off sparks when he was angry. At times he could be quite easygoing, but more often he was quick to anger. And when Thor was angry, he was a flaming terror.

There was one member of the family of gods who liked to bait Thor. His name was Loki. He was really a giant, and related to the gods only by marriage. At heart, Loki was not on the side of the gods. He had a vicious streak in him and often caused them trouble. One night Loki went too far. He played a cruel trick on Thor's wife, Sif.

———◆———

Thor's wife had the most beautiful hair in Asgard. One night while she was asleep, Loki cut her golden hair close to its roots. Sif ran in tears to Thor.

Thor looked at Sif with amazement and then with fury. All that remained of her flowing hair was a golden fuzz. Lightning flashed from his eyes. His fiery-red beard bristled and the sparks crackled. His red hair stood up like flames of fire. He was a terrifying sight. He sucked in enough air to blow a gale and boomed out a name like a clap of thunder, "Loki!"

Thor knew it could be no one but Loki, and he set out to find him. When Loki heard him coming, he started to run. But Thor soon caught Loki and grabbed him by the throat.

Gasping, Loki swore that he would somehow give back Sif's hair. Thor loosened his grip for a moment to let Loki explain. Loki knew how to talk his way out of a tight spot. Besides, he had a good idea.

"I'll have one of the dwarfs make a wig of gold for Sif," said Loki. "The magic wig will become real hair as soon as it touches Sif's head, and she'll have long, golden hair again. Thor, you have my sacred promise."

Thor considered it. He would know where to find Loki if he failed to keep his promise. He gave Loki a final shake and let him go.

Loki was still in trouble. He could probably have the wig made for Sif, but he was afraid the gods would not easily forgive this latest prank of his. And so, Loki thought of a way to win back their favor.

After the dwarf had made a wig out of fine strands of gold, Loki decided to have him make presents for Odin and for the god of sunshine, Frey. For Odin, Loki had a magic spear made that would never miss its mark. Odin would forgive almost anything for such a present. And for Frey, Loki had the dwarf make a wonderful ship — a ship that could sail on the waters or fly through the air. The magic ship could be made large enough to hold an army, or could fold small enough to fit into a pocket.

Loki was proud of his presents for the gods, and he boasted about them to the other dwarfs. A dwarf named Brock heard him — he could hardly help hearing him, for Loki had a loud voice.

Brock listened to Loki for as long as he could stand it. Finally Brock said that Loki's presents were nothing to boast about.

"You've heard of my brother Sindri?" Brock asked.

"The blacksmith?" Loki asked scornfully.

"He's more than a blacksmith. He's a goldsmith, a silversmith — an artisan. He can make finer presents than you could ever dream of," Brock answered angrily.

Loki laughed. He held up the gold wig and the spear and the ship. "Your brother can make finer presents than these?" he asked, almost believing he had made the presents himself. "We'll have a contest and let the gods decide whether Sindri can create such wonders as these."

In the heat of the argument Loki shouted at Brock, "I'll bet my head against yours that Sindri can't make anything to equal my presents."

"That's a bet," Brock agreed grimly.

Brock went to his brother and told him about the contest. Sindri was sure they could win. But he warned Brock to take care that the fire in the forge was always very hot. Sindri piled fuel on the fire as Brock pumped air into it with the bellows to keep it hot. Meanwhile, Loki had hidden himself in the shadows of the cave and was watching the dwarfs.

Sindri first made a wild boar out of gold. This remarkable animal could fly at amazing speed, bearing a god on its back. At night, golden beams would shine from its bristles and light the way.

Sindri was now ready to start on the second present. While he went to get some more gold, Brock continued to pump the bellows. The minute Sindri had left, Loki changed himself into a gadfly and stung Brock's hands. Brock yelled, but he held fast to the bellows.

When Sindri returned, he put some of the gold in the forge — just a little bit this time. Loki, still disguised as a gadfly, flew closer so he could overhear the dwarfs' conversation.

"The second present is going to be a ring. Not an ordinary ring, no indeed!" Sindri said. "This ring will create life. Not only will it make the crops grow, but this ring will even make babies grow. And to prove its great power, the ring will create eight new rings, every ninth night. Keep working the bellows," he told Brock as he left to get more supplies. "The fire must be very hot."

Loki flew at Brock again. This time, Loki stung the dwarf's face. Brock screamed with pain, but he still held on to the bellows.

Sindri returned, carrying a heavy, solid mass and grunting under its weight. Loki buzzed over the brothers to find out what it was.

"Iron," Sindri told Brock. The dwarf took the ring out of the forge and put the iron in. "This time I shall make a hammer — but what a hammer! A god will be able to throw it at anything, anywhere, and it will come right back into his hand. The hammer will be small enough to fit into a belt, but when it is thrown it will swell to the size of a house. A god will be able to smash anything or anybody with this hammer; then it will return to him, small and handy."

Loki became alarmed, for he knew Thor would want

that hammer. The magic hammer might win the contest. If it did, what would become of Loki? He would lose his head. Loki wondered why he had been fool enough to bet his head.

"Brock, keep the fire red-hot. Don't stop working the bellows. Not for a second," Sindri warned. Then he concentrated on the magic while Brock busily pumped the bellows.

Loki flew right at Brock's eyes and stung him with a fury. Brock howled and finally let go of the bellows, just long enough to brush the gadfly away.

When Sindri drew the hammer out, he examined it carefully. "The handle is too short," he complained. "It's your fault, Brock! You shouldn't have let go of the bellows, even for that brief moment." But still it was a powerful magic hammer.

The next day, Brock and Loki took their presents to the gods. The gods knew of Loki's sacred promise to Thor, and they settled this matter first. The wig became Sif's own golden hair as soon as it was placed on her head. Loki had made good his promise, but the gods felt it was the least he should have done.

The contest began in earnest when Loki and Brock showed the other presents to the gods. Each present brought sounds of approval.

The instant Thor saw the hammer, he seized it and threw it. The hammer grew big, smashed a hole in a mountain, then became small, and returned right back to his hand. What a weapon! It could strike a giant as big as an iceberg and smash him into a thousand

snowflakes. Thor thundered his praise, and the other gods agreed that nothing could surpass this wonderful hammer. The dwarf won the contest.

As soon as Loki heard that Brock had won, he fled from Asgard. If Brock wanted Loki's head, he would have to catch him first. The dwarf could not run as fast as Loki. But Thor could! He ran after Loki and brought him back.

Payment of a debt was an affair of honor. Besides, Thor had had enough of Loki. Let the dwarf cut his head off; Loki deserved no mercy.

Loki's clever mind worked fast as he spoke to the gods. "All right, I've promised to pay with my head.

But Brock had better remember one thing, I didn't bet my neck — not one little piece of it." He turned to Brock and said, "Go ahead, take my head. You won it. But you'd better not lay your greedy hands on my neck."

The gods laughed. They had to agree that Loki's neck was still his and he did not owe any part of it to Brock.

Brock stood firmly by his claim. "Well, Loki, I still own your head. It's mine, and I'm going to sew your mouth shut."

Brock borrowed an awl from his brother and sewed Loki's mouth shut. The gods teased Loki, knowing he could not answer back. But eventually he found a way to undo the stitches. Who could shut Loki up for long?

Thor's Visit to Jotunheim

Thor had heard many complaints about the cold winds from Jotunheim. The long, cold winters were bad enough, but icy winds came back after spring had already started. The giants would wait until the first tender leaves had pushed through the soil and the buds had peeped from the bushes and trees. Then they sent frosty winds to wither the newborn green.

The time had come for the gods and the giants to settle their many differences. The unseasonable winds gave Thor an excuse to go to Jotunheim. Now that he had his magic hammer, he would take it along to prove that the gods were more powerful than the giants.

Thor decided to take Loki with him. He was sure Loki would behave himself. After all, it was not too long ago that Brock had sewn up Loki's mouth. Ever since then, Loki thought twice before causing any trouble for the gods. Besides, Thor believed Loki might be useful.

Loki had come from Jotunheim and knew what to expect of the giants. The giants would probably put the strength of the gods to a test by holding games. Loki warned Thor that they had a tricky way of playing.

By some mysterious means, the giants knew of Thor's plan to visit Utgard, a city in the land of the giants. They had heard all about Thor's magic hammer and were curious to test not only the might of the gods but also the might of the hammer. The Giant King, named Utgard-loki, prepared for the interesting visitor from Asgard in the tricky manner of the giants.

———————————•———————————

Thor and Loki crossed the Rainbow Bridge and left Asgard. The first night they stopped at a farmhouse in Midgard to ask for food and shelter. The farmer was not rich, but he was proud of his fine family. He had a son, Thialfi, who could run as fast as the wind. Thor spoke with the youth and liked his spirit and courage. The great runner might be useful in the games, and Thor decided to take Thialfi with him to Jotunheim.

On the second night, Thor, Loki, and Thialfi lost their way. The night was pitch black, and they stumbled into what they thought was the open doorway of a house. It seemed an odd house, but they were in an unfamiliar land and strange things were to be expected. They were cold, and the house — or whatever it was — offered shelter. There was no furniture, so they lay down on the floor and fell fast asleep.

During the night, the house shook and there was a rumbling sound. They thought it was an earthquake, but there was no use running out into the black night. They were safer inside.

The next morning Thor awoke and thought he saw a mountain next to the house. It was not a mountain, though. It was a giant. The giant opened one sleepy eye and asked, "Where's my other glove?"

Looking over his shoulder, Thor realized they had mistaken the giant's glove for a house. Thor, Loki, and Thialfi had spent the night in the giant's glove! Thor reached for his hammer. But the giant gave him a warning look, and Thor prudently left the hammer in his belt.

"Good morning," the god said politely. "May I ask your name?"

"My name is Skrymir. I don't have to ask yours," the giant said, noticing the hammer. "That hammer tells me who you are."

Thor admitted he was the god of thunder and said he was on a journey to Utgard, the city of the Giant King, in Jotunheim.

"Then let's go part of the way together," the giant suggested.

Thor glanced at Loki. They could see no reason to refuse. It was agreed that Thor, Loki, Thialfi, and the giant would continue the journey together. Thor and his companions gathered their provisions. They had a knapsack filled with food, and Thialfi was having trouble getting the heavy load strapped onto his back.

"Why don't we put all the food into my knapsack?" the giant suggested. "I can easily carry it."

Thor could hardly refuse such a generous offer, so he agreed to that, too.

He soon wished the giant had not invited himself along. Skrymir walked ahead with giant strides. Thor, Loki, and Thialfi ran until their tongues hung out. But it was useless trying to keep up with the giant.

Toward evening they finally caught up with Skrymir, who had decided to stop for the night. He had picked a spot beside a huge mountain and was stretched out asleep under an oak tree. The knapsack had been tossed on the ground beside him.

Thor and his companions were hungry, and they

eagerly snatched at the knapsack. Thor pulled and pulled at the knot, but he could not untie it. Thor was furious.

He was about to knock the giant on the head with his hammer when the giant opened his eyes, stretched out comfortably, and asked, "Have you had your supper yet?"

Thor refused to admit he could not untie the knapsack. He grumbled, "Why yes! We've just finished eating."

Hungry and in a bad humor, Thor and his companions decided to get some sleep. Thor was just dozing off when a terrible noise woke him. He knew it was not an earthquake this time. It was the giant's snoring! Thor muttered and rolled over. It was no use; he could not sleep. The giant snored louder and louder.

Thor sat up and said, "That's the last straw! Today that miserable giant walked so fast that I nearly wore my legs off trying to keep up with him. As for the knapsack, he deliberately tied it so tight that I'd have to go without supper. I'm hungry as a lion and tired as a . . . ." Thor was interrupted by a loud, ear-splitting snore.

He sprang up and hurled his hammer at the giant's head. WHOOSH——CRASH!!

The giant woke up. He slowly raised his hand to his head and removed a twig. "This must have fallen from the tree," the giant remarked mildly, and rolling over, went back to sleep.

Thor was dumbfounded. What was the meaning of this? A blow from his powerful hammer and the giant rolled over and went back to sleep! The giant began to snore again. In a double fury, Thor flung the hammer at

him! Again the giant woke up, put his hand to his head, and complained that a leaf or something from the tree had dropped on him.

Thor shook his head as he turned the hammer over and over in his hands. He was bewildered and began to feel very uneasy about his visit to Utgard.

The next morning, Skrymir showed Thor the road leading to Utgard and then left to go his own way. Thor did not bother to ask the giant where he was going. He had enough on his mind. If Skrymir was a sample of the Utgard giants, then Thor had reason to worry. But more discouraging than anything else, his magic hammer, the weapon he had been counting on most of all, had let him down last night.

Thor, Loki, and Thialfi arrived in Utgard and found the gates of the city locked. But the gates were so huge that the gods could fit between the bars. They slipped through them and boldly stood before Utgard-loki, the Giant King. Utgard-loki looked familiar, but one giant looked exactly like another to Thor.

The great giant was amused, and pretended to be surprised to find the gods so small. He deliberately embarrassed them by saying that only small, stray animals ever managed to squeeze through the gates of

the city. Just as Thor expected—for Loki had warned him—the Giant King suggested that the visit begin with a contest.

"Well, Thor, what can you and your companions do best?" Utgard-loki asked in his most cordial manner.

Loki had a quick answer. "If you want to see who can eat the most, I'm your man. I'll challenge anybody." It had been a long time since Loki had eaten, and he felt a powerful hunger.

"Excellent! An eating contest might be a good way to start the games," Utgard-loki agreed.

The contest was between Loki and Logi the cook. The Giant King had a huge trough filled with meat brought to them. Loki started eating at one end of the trough, and Logi started at the other end. By the time they both reached the middle of the trough, Loki had eaten half the meat. But he did not win, nor was the contest a tie.

"Why, Loki, you've eaten only the meat and left the bones!" the giant pointed out. "Now Logi's eaten not only his half of the meat, including the bones, but half of the trough as well! I'm afraid the gods have lost the first game," the giant decided, giving Thor a sly smile.

Thor was annoyed. He hated having his side lose, especially since the gods were trying to prove that they were more powerful than the giants.

Utgard-loki made an effort to be polite. "Thor, I'm sure you can do better than Loki. What do you do best?"

"I'll challenge anyone to a drinking contest. I can drain the biggest cup in one gulp, and I dare any giant to match me!" thundered Thor boldly.

Utgard-loki had a drinking horn brought to Thor. It was filled to the brim with water.

"A good drinker can drain this horn in one gulp," Utgard-loki said. "A fair drinker can do it in two. But if anyone needs more than two gulps to empty the horn, we think he's pretty poor as drinkers go."

The horn was very long, but not so long, the god thought, that he could not drain it in one swallow. Thor tilted the horn and drank. He drank until he thought he would burst. He had to stop. But when he looked into the horn, it was still filled almost to the brim.

42

"Maybe you're just not thirsty," Utgard-loki suggested.

Thor knew the giant was baiting him. He glared back at Utgard-loki, and raising the drinking horn, took a long, deep gulp. He glanced out of the corner of his eye at the giant and saw that he looked worried.

At last Thor put the horn down. He felt certain that he had emptied it this time. But it was still filled to within an inch of the brim.

"Only an inch?" Utgard-loki asked, now pleased with himself.

Thor gripped the drinking horn once more. "I'll empty it this time," he muttered to himself, "or I'll drown trying." He almost did drown, but he failed to empty the horn.

It was now Thialfi's turn. The giant smiled at him and asked, "Is it true you're a racer? Pretty fast, are you?"

"Try him," Thor answered irritably.

"All right. We have a runner here—his name's Hugi." The giant paused to see whether the name meant anything to Thor, but Thor's attention and hopes were all on Thialfi. "Well, we'll see," said Utgard-loki finally.

Hugi and Thialfi took their places. The instant the race started, Hugi was ahead—so far ahead that he was way out of Thialfi's sight. His feet were like wings on the wind. Hugi went all around the racing course and flashed ahead of Thialfi again.

"The gods lose another contest! But that was a pretty good try," Utgard-loki said.

Thor did not reply. He looked grim.

"I'll tell you what, I'd like to give you a chance to win at something," Utgard-loki suggested, trying not to laugh. "We have a little game—to tell the truth, my children play it. We call it 'Lifting Kitty off the Ground.' Kitty is my little cat there."

Thor was trying to control his temper. His jaw was set, his beard stiff. He looked at the cat. It was not little. It was the biggest cat—if it was a cat—that he had ever seen. He wondered whether cats could be so different in Jotunheim.

"The trick is to get all four paws off the ground," the giant said. "Kitty doesn't like to be moved. You know how cats are."

Thor was still staring at the big animal. It looked mean.

"Kitty digs her claws into the ground to get a firm grip," the giant explained. He saw the look on Thor's face and asked, "You aren't afraid of cats, are you?"

Thor refused to admit that he was afraid of a cat. He went over to the big animal, and it spat at him. He reached a hand under the animal to lift it, and it hissed and spat and dug its claws into the ground. Thor pulled and grunted, and the animal's body stretched. He pulled again.

"He's pulled a paw loose!" said one of the giants, as if it were really remarkable.

Remarkable or not, it was the best Thor could do. The animal gripped the ground hard, and Thor could not loosen the other three paws.

"Kitty wins!" Utgard-loki announced gleefully.

"Enough of your children's games. Who wants to wrestle?" Thor said fiercely.

The giant rubbed his chin. Thor could see that Utgard-loki was enjoying himself. "A wrestling match would be embarrassing, Thor. I don't have anybody who would want to wrestle with such a little god." He pretended to think it over. "Oh, well, there's an old nurse—her name is Elli. Our children like to wrestle with Elli, and...."

Thor started to object, but Elli was already standing

in front of him. He tried to shove her aside. Elli grabbed his arms and began wrestling with him. Thor tried to slip out of her grip, and found he could not move. Then, before he knew what had happened, the mighty Thor found himself down on one knee. Elli had thrown him.

"She wins. Elli wins," Utgard-loki announced with a hearty laugh. The giant was feeling good. He clapped his huge hands together and rubbed them briskly. "Had enough? I think we've had enough games. What do you say?"

"There doesn't seem to be much point in going on with these contests," admitted Thor, for he had had enough.

The following morning, Utgard-loki went with Thor, Loki, and Thialfi to the gate of the city. He led them beyond the gates and pointed the way back to Asgard.

"Before you leave, Thor, I'd like to know if you've proved what you'd hoped to prove by your visit," Utgard-loki said.

"I don't feel the gods have shown how great and mighty they really are. But if you think the gods are weak," Thor warned, "that would be your mistake."

The giant chuckled. "Now that the official visit is over, Thor, I'll let you in on a few secrets." Utgard-loki could not help gloating over the way he had tricked the gods. "I was the giant you met on the way here. I told you my name was Skrymir. When you threw your hammer at me, you didn't know that I had moved a mountain to protect my head." He pointed to the mountain. "Just look at the ditch you made in it with your hammer."

Thor saw the gully that ran from the top of the mountain to the bottom.

"You might have made a crease like that in my head," he complained, shaking his big finger at Thor as though he were scolding a naughty child. "You ought to be more careful with your little hammer."

Thor fumed. Little hammer, was it!

"And I'm sorry you didn't have your supper that night," the giant continued. Thor started to say something, but the giant held up his hand. "Oh, I knew you didn't have any supper." A chuckle rumbled in the giant's chest. He was having a good time at Thor's expense. "You couldn't get the knapsack open because I tied it with a special kind of iron. You've heard of troll iron?"

So it was iron from the dwarfs! Thor had heard of it, but he did not say anything. He was beginning to lose his temper.

"As for the contests," the giant went on, "I have to admit you tried hard, all of you. Loki, for instance, ate like a hog. He really made a pig of himself, but he didn't have a chance against my cook Logi. Didn't you guess who Logi was? No, I can see you didn't. Logi is Wildfire."

Thor glared at the giant and said nothing.

"Wildfire can consume just about anything—that is, if he is hot enough. And Logi was really hot. He ate the trough, the bones. . . . You didn't know Logi was Wildfire?" he asked innocently.

If Thor had answered the giant, his anger would have flared out of control. Utgard-loki had defeated the gods by trickery and foul play. He would laugh all the harder if Thor showed the giant that he was boiling with rage.

"And when you were drinking out of that horn, didn't you know . . . ?" Utgard-loki stopped, and stroking his chin, grinned. "No, I guess you didn't."

"All right, I didn't know. What was it?" Thor asked, still trying to control his temper.

"Why, only that the other end of the horn was dipped into the ocean," Utgard-loki said, pointing toward the ocean. "Just look how much you drank! My, my! Look how far the water is from the shoreline. You caused an ebb tide." The giant pretended to be serious, and added, "You really must have been thirsty."

Without thinking, Thor reached for his hammer. The giant paused, watching for Thor's next move. Thor's hand rested on the hammer, and Utgard-loki continued talking, never once taking his eyes from Thor's hammer.

"And that race Thialfi had with Hugi! You know, that little boy can really run. But to race against Hugi he'd

have to run faster than thought. That's who Hugi is, he's Thought." Utgard-loki pointed to Thialfi and said, "I wish he could have seen himself. He was really running.

"As for the cat," Utgard-loki continued, "well, he isn't a cat at all. He's the Midgard serpent. He's so long that he dips into the sea and wraps himself around Midgard, the earth."

By this time, Thor's curiosity was aroused even more than his temper. "Who was that old woman?" he demanded stiffly.

"The one you wrestled with?" the giant asked. "Why, Thor, that was Old Age. Let me give you a bit of advice. A man makes a fool of himself when he tries to fight off Old Age."

Thor drew out his hammer, but the giant grabbed his wrist. And when Utgard-loki spoke again, he was no longer teasing Thor.

"Now let me give you another bit of advice. Stay away from Jotunheim. I admit the gods are dangerous, especially you with your hammer. But the giants are dangerous, too. If you ever come this way again, I'll cut you down in your tracks," he said gruffly.

Thor's anger exploded. With a violent effort, he pulled away from the giant and raised his hammer. But the giant had already disappeared. Thor swung around to throw the hammer at the castle and smash it with a single blow. But he suddenly stopped, unable to believe his eyes.

Where was the castle? Nowhere—it had suddenly vanished into a frosty mist.

Frey Wins
a Bride and Loses
His Famous Sword

Of all the gods in Asgard, the most pleasing to look upon was Frey, the god of sunshine and rain. Frey made the sun bright and warm, but not so hot that it scorched the land. When he sent the rains, they were gentle and neither flooded nor beat down the farmers' crops.

Yet one day while Odin was gone from Asgard, this gentle god did a rash thing. He sat on Odin's throne. No one had ever dared to take Odin's place. Frey was certain to be punished for it. In a way, he was.

From Odin's throne, Frey could see beyond the earth to the frosty land of the giants. There, in Jotunheim, he saw Gerda, the beautiful giant maiden, and fell in love with her. The giantess would refuse his love because he was a god and because she came from a proud family of

giants. Although he knew his love was doomed, Frey
could hardly eat or sleep for thinking of Gerda.

Now when the god of sunshine and rain leaves his
work to pine and sulk, he is missed very much. Without
sunshine and rain, what would become of the world?
So while the gentle god of weather pined away, the crops
perished.

Frey had a helper named Skirnir. At last, Frey's father
sent Skirnir to discover the cause of Frey's sadness.

Skirnir found Frey beside a stream. The messenger
asked him why he suffered alone. Frey could no longer
keep silent. He confided to Skirnir, "I can't eat or sleep,
or make the sun shine or the rain fall, until the daughter
of Gymir promises to be my wife. Gerda is the cause of
my suffering."

"If you'll lend me your horse to go through the magic
fire, I'll go to Jotunheim for you," said Skirnir. "I'll
speak to this maid and tell her of your love. Nothing will
be gained by sulking and pining away, my friend and
master."

"The journey to Jotunheim is dangerous and you may
be killed," Frey said. "Take my horse or anything that
will help you to win this proud giantess for me."

Skirnir saw a chance to bargain for something he had
always secretly wanted — Frey's famous sword. This
sword could fight by itself, if necessary.

"I'll need a weapon to defend myself when I am among
the enemy giants," Skirnir told Frey.

"What kind of weapon?" Frey asked, moodily staring
into the stream.

"I promise to win the giantess for you if you'll give me your famous sword," said Skirnir boldly.

Frey looked up at Skirnir and hesitated. Then he said, "Take it, take it. Only be sure you bring back her promise to be my wife." He knew that he would bitterly regret giving away his sword.

As Skirnir turned to leave, he noticed that the god's handsome face was reflected in the stream. He stooped to gather the reflection in his drinking horn, and set out for Jotunheim.

On the way to Gymir's castle, Skirnir met a shepherd. The shepherd warned him that the castle was protected by a wall of fire. But Frey's horse could plunge through fire, and so Skirnir rode quickly on his way.

He soon arrived at Gymir's castle and safely crossed
the flaming barrier. Then Skirnir was attacked by huge,
howling dogs. But the magic sword drove them off.

The shepherd had told Skirnir in what part of the
castle the beautiful giantess lived. Skirnir saw a light in
Gerda's room, and soon the maiden heard the hooves of
Skirnir's horse outside her window. She thought he must
be an important visitor and sent a servant to bring him
to her.

Gerda was as proud as she was beautiful. When Skirnir
told her why he had come to Jotunheim, she was angry.
"The giants and the gods gain nothing by marriage. Our
gains are made on the battlefield. I am the daughter of
a proud family. Gymir's daughter marry a god? Never!"

Skirnir showed her the reflection of the handsome god,
which was still in his drinking horn. Gerda ignored it.
Skirnir offered her presents. She scorned them. Then he
tried to frighten her. He drew the magic sword and said,
"If you don't come with me, I may cut off your head."

"You'll be lucky if my father doesn't cut you into small
pieces," she replied coolly.

Skirnir was not stopped by Gerda's pride. He had
brought a magic wand with him. This was his last chance.
If he failed to charm the beautiful giantess with his magic
wand, Gymir would certainly have him slain. This mission
to win Gerda's love for Frey must not fail. He rubbed
the wand and raised it over Gerda's head, tapping the
air three times.

Her pride yielded to the magic. "Tell your noble master
I shall meet him in the beautiful forest of Barri. Bid

Frey meet me there on the evening of the ninth day," she said. The magic of the gods was so much stronger than Gerda's pride that her heart was filled with love for the handsome Frey.

Frey was wildly happy when Skirnir returned with the message from Gerda. He wanted to be with the beautiful giantess that very moment.

"How can I wait so long?" he asked.

"It's only nine days," Skirnir reminded him.

"No, Skirnir," Frey said. "It will seem like nine long months of winter to me."

The evening of the ninth day came at last. Frey did meet Gerda in the beautiful forest of Barri. Soon the god married the giantess. Skirnir won the magic sword — the sword that Frey would need on the day of the last battle between the gods and the giants.

How the Gods Chained the Fenris Wolf

Loki had three children, the Midgard serpent, Hela, and Fenrir. Loki's children were monsters — and dreadful ones, at that!

One of Loki's children, the wolf Fenrir, was famous for his fierceness and strength, although he was still quite young. He was known as the Fenris wolf.

There was a prophecy, or perhaps only a rumor, that the Fenris wolf would someday eat one of the gods. According to the prophecy, it would be Odin. Naturally, Odin was curious to see the wolf, and he sent for Fenrir.

The Fenris wolf was not yet full-grown. But since he already looked so fierce and evil, the gods advised Odin to have him killed at once.

But the wolf was one of Loki's children and Loki was

Odin's half-brother. "We'll keep Fenrir chained here, where we can watch him," Odin decided.

The gods insisted the monster was a danger and threat to them and that he should be killed. But Odin ordered them to chain the wolf and asked Tyr, the god of war, to keep a close watch over him and feed him.

The gods forged a chain and then approached Fenrir, pretending to play a game. "Here's a chain, Fenrir," one of them said to the snarling wolf. "Let's see if you're strong enough to break it."

Fenrir was not fooled. He was aware that the gods wanted to keep him tied up, but he knew he could break this chain. The wolf smiled to himself and allowed the gods to chain him. When the gods had finished, Fenrir broke the chain easily.

The gods looked at one another. The wolf watched them, his wild eyes waiting to see what they would try next.

"You're a strong wolf," one of the gods said, with an uneasy smile. "I'm sure you can break a chain twice as thick as this one."

"Maybe I can, and maybe I can't. But that's no affair of yours, is it?" Fenrir said, and he lay down and pretended to ignore them.

The gods forged a chain of hard iron, twice as thick and three times as strong as the first one. When they returned with the new chain, the wolf sprang up and snarled at them.

"It's only a game," one of the gods said. "We just want to see if you can break this one, too."

Fenrir looked at the chain and laughed to himself. Once again the gods tied him. Then the wolf stretched his powerful shoulders, and the chain flew apart, almost as quickly as the first one had.

This time the gods looked at one another with alarm. It was clear that no ordinary chain would bind Fenrir. The gods held a conference, and they all agreed to take their problem to the dwarfs.

These homely beings understood the deep mysteries of nature. They combined skill and magic to create the most unusual things. So the dwarfs agreed to make a special kind of chain for the gods to use to bind the Fenris wolf.

They gathered the roots of a mountain, the spittle of birds, the beards of women, the breath of fish, and the sound of a cat walking. And that, the Norse people say, is why, to this day, mountains have no roots, birds no spittle, women no beards, fish no breath, and the step of a cat makes no sound.

The dwarfs mixed roots and spittle, a wisp of beard, a dash of breath, a pinch of sound, and made a chain as fine as silk. When the wolf saw the chain, so fine that it

could barely be seen, he eyed the gods warily. He knew
that it must be some trick, and he allowed the gods to tie
him on only one condition.

"To prove your good faith, one of you will have to
leave his hand in my mouth. If this is a trick, then I will
bite off the hand," he said.

The gods all looked at Tyr. As the god of war, it was
up to Tyr to take such risks. Without hesitating, Tyr
placed his hand in the wolf's mouth.

The gods tied the wolf with the soft, silklike chain.
Fenrir struggled to break loose. The harder he tried, the
tighter the filmy chain bound him.

Fenrir wanted to remind the gods of their promise. But if he opened his mouth, then Tyr's hand would be free. Fenrir knew then that he had been tricked. So he bit off Tyr's hand, and that is why the god of war had only one hand.

The gods took one end of the chain and tied it around a big rock. They buried the rock deep in the ground and rolled another big boulder on top of it. The wolf snarled, and his mouth dripped with foam. In a blind rage he bit

at everything in sight — he chewed the chain, he bit the rock, he snapped at the gods.

Just as Fenrir opened his mouth wide, showing his sharp, jagged teeth, one of the gods jammed a sword between his jaws! The Fenris wolf could not bite or snap at the gods now.

Someday Fenrir would have his revenge, and the prophecy would come true. But Fenrir would have a long wait ahead of him.

The Eagle and the Golden Apples

In Asgard there lived a lovely goddess named Idun. She was loved for herself and cherished for her basket of golden apples. They were wonderful apples, for they kept the gods young. Her supply was endless. Each time she gave a god one of her apples, a new one appeared in the basket.

Idun had never refused an apple to a god. But it was known that she had to give them willingly for the charm to work. It would not keep anyone young who stole an apple or took them by force.

The gods did not try to stop Idun from going with her basket wherever she liked. But they did try to guard her from strangers. If she or her basket were lost, the gods would have to grow old.

Idun and her apples were almost lost because of Loki.

———◆———

One day as Odin, Loki, and Hoenir were walking in Midgard, they came upon a herd of oxen. The gods had

been walking for a long time and had not eaten. They were hungry, and Loki decided to kill one of the oxen for their supper. The gods built a blazing fire and put the ox on the flames to cook.

"It is time to take the ox out of the fire," Loki announced after a while. "It has been in the fire long enough."

The gods began to eat but found that the ox was not cooked at all. This seemed strange, for the fire was blazing hot. The gods put the ox in the fire for another hour.

At the end of the hour, Loki was half starved. He tested the meat. It was still raw! Loki looked at Odin in amazement, but Odin himself was baffled.

"Hasn't it cooked yet?" asked Hoenir, seeing their puzzled looks.

"No," replied a strange voice, "because I will not let the fire cook the ox."

The gods looked up and saw a giant-sized eagle perched on the branch of a tree.

"The eagle must have some secret power, some magic

way of drawing the heat from the fire," Loki whispered to the others.

"I'll cook the ox on one condition. You must give me a share of it," the eagle said.

By this time, the gods were so hungry they agreed to share the ox with the eagle. The eagle swooped down and fanned the fire with his wings. The ox cooked in a matter of minutes. But before the gods could stop the eagle, he tore off the hind and front parts of the ox.

The eagle was about to fly away when Loki picked up a stout branch and gave him a swat. The branch stuck to the eagle's back. Loki tried to let go of the branch, but his hands were stuck fast. The eagle flew over sharp

rocks and thorny briars, dragging Loki over them. Loki begged for mercy.

"You won't get any mercy from me," the eagle said, "unless you promise to do what I ask."

"I'll promise," Loki yelled as he scraped his knee on a rock. "What is it you want?"

"I want the golden apples," the eagle told him.

"What apples?" Loki gasped, pretending not to know.

"You know 'what apples'! I want the golden apples of youth. I want Idun's apples."

"The gods never let Idun out of their sight," said Loki.

"Loki, you know you can get Idun out of Asgard," the eagle insisted.

"Impossible! How can I?" wailed Loki.

"You must work it out. You have a clever tongue. Think of some excuse. Just get Idun to a forest and leave her there, alone!"

"All right," Loki agreed in agony. "Now will you stop dragging me around?"

"Not until you take a god's oath on your promise," demanded the eagle.

"I give you my sacred oath," said Loki.

The eagle was satisfied. Loki would never dare to break a god's oath.

When Loki found his way back to Odin and Hoenir, he did not tell them about his promise to the eagle. Loki was up to his old tricks again.

As soon as he returned to Asgard, Loki thought of a way to kidnap Idun. He told her of a forest that had golden apples exactly like hers.

"There can be no apples like mine," she said.

"Come with me and I'll show you," Loki insisted. "Take your apples along, and we'll compare them."

Idun went with Loki to the forest, bringing her basket of apples with her. The god left her there alone.

In a short time the eagle came, snatched up Idun, and flew with her to his castle. He changed into the storm giant Thjazi and asked Idun for her apples. She refused. Thjazi threatened her, but his threats could not persuade Idun to give him the apples.

Back in Asgard, Odin was beginning to feel his age. He had not seen Idun in a while and wondered where she was. The other gods had been looking for her, too, and remembered seeing her last with Loki.

Odin sent for Loki. It didn't take long to get the truth out of him. Odin learned what had happened to Idun.

"If you don't bring Idun back, the penalty will be death. And you don't have much time," Odin warned him sternly.

Loki remembered that the goddess Freya possessed the wings of a falcon. He went to Freya, and she lent him the falcon wings. With them he was able to turn into a falcon and fly to Jotunheim.

Loki found Idun walking in the castle garden. He quickly changed her into a nut and flew off with her.

Meanwhile, Thjazi, who was fishing in a nearby stream, saw the falcon fly from his garden toward Asgard. Thjazi became an eagle again and flew after Loki.

Loki knew the eagle could fly faster than he could. If the eagle caught him before he reached Asgard, it would

mean his death. The eagle was drawing closer and closer. Loki flapped the falcon wings so fast and hard that his heart almost burst.

Loki, too, had grown old. In his haste to get Idun away from the giant's castle, there had not been time to eat one of her apples. It was too late now. He had changed them, along with Idun, into the nut he held in his claw. Loki glanced back and saw the eagle gaining fast.

The eagle and the falcon approached Asgard. The gods recognized Thjazi and Loki, and began to rake together a mound of wood shavings near the walls of the city. The eagle reached out his claw, just inches away from Loki. With a final spurt of energy, Loki was safely over the walls. The eagle Thjazi had lost his prey. And Idun and her magic apples were once more in the hands of the gods.

Once Idun and Loki were safely inside the walls, the gods set the wood shavings on fire. The flames flared up, and just as Thjazi flew over them, his wings caught fire. Down came Thjazi with a crash!

The aging gods gathered around Idun. They eagerly took the apples and ate them. Their wrinkled faces became smooth, their bent bodies straightened, and once again

the gods were young. Because they felt so good, they felt generous. They even pitied the dead eagle.

"Thjazi wanted to be young," said Odin. "But only the gods can stay young."

"Yes," Thor agreed. "But it seems hard to blame him for wanting the youth of the gods."

"Look at his eyes," Odin said. "The hope for youth still shines in them. Let's give Thjazi immortality. I will change his eyes into stars."

Odin plucked out the fiery-bright eyes and threw them into the sky. From that time, the two stars were known as the Eyes of Thjazi.

Even the Stones Weep for Balder

Balder, the son of Frigga and Odin, was a god who deserved to be loved by all. He was kind and generous, and he was always happy. He was known as the god of light. All who knew Balder loved him—everyone except Loki. But then, Loki loved no one.

A time came when the god of light became sad and depressed. Frigga and Odin wondered what had caused Balder's sudden sadness. They finally persuaded him to tell them the reason.

Balder had been having bad dreams. When he awoke in the morning, he could not remember his dreams. But the dreams must have been frightful, for they made him feel sad all day.

In Asgard, dreams were taken seriously. Dreams had special meanings, and bad dreams meant something was gravely wrong. Frigga feared that a dreadful misfortune would come to her son.

One day Frigga tried to make sure that Balder would be protected from any evil deed. The goddess sent her servants to everybody and everything that lived in the land of the gods. The servants spoke to the gods, to the animals and the plants, to the sticks and the stones— they spoke to everybody and everything that might harm Balder. Every living thing promised to protect Balder. Then the servants returned to Frigga.

"You talked to everybody and everything?" the goddess asked them.

"Yes. Balder will now be protected," they all answered at once.

One of the servants suddenly remembered something. "There was a tender little mistletoe that grew on the branch of an oak. Only the oak promised. I forgot to ask the little mistletoe. But no harm can come from the sweet mistletoe."

Frigga agreed. "You're quite right. The mistletoe is too tender and small to harm anybody," she said, relieved that Balder was now safe.

During this time, Odin was away on a long journey. He had gone to a strange land to learn the meaning of Balder's dreams. It was a dangerous journey, across the shaky bridge between life and death into the realm of

Hela, goddess of the dead. Odin found the people of Hel making preparations for a new arrival.

"To judge by your preparations, you must be expecting a god or someone of great fame," Odin said.

"Yes, indeed," Hela replied. "We are preparing for Balder's arrival."

"But he is not dead," Odin said.

"We know this. He will die soon, by his brother Hod's hand," said Hela solemnly.

When Odin returned to Asgard, Frigga told him all that she had done to protect Balder. Odin was relieved to hear this, in spite of what he had learned from Hela.

"How could Hod kill Balder?" he asked himself. It seemed most unlikely. Not only was he Balder's brother, but Hod was blind, for he was the god of darkness.

Time went by. No one had harmed Balder in any way. One day a god threw a small stone at Balder, a stone that had promised not to hurt him. The god just wanted to see what would happen. The stone did not hit Balder. It kept its promise. The god tried a bigger stone, and that refused to hit him, too. Then he tried a blunted spear. The spear curved away and missed Balder, just as the stones had.

It soon became a new game. The gods spent many a pleasant afternoon throwing their weapons at Balder and watching them curve away from him. Balder enjoyed the game, too. He liked to see the gods enjoy themselves and did not mind playing the target for their spears. Everyone felt that Balder was perfectly safe.

There was only one god besides Hod who did not take part in the games. He was Loki. Unlike the other gods, he hated Balder. Surely, the evil god thought, something can harm him.

Loki found out about the tender young mistletoe. It was the only living thing in Asgard that had not promised to safeguard Balder. Loki went to the mistletoe, and with magic, forced it to grow tall and strong. He cut it down and made a deadly spear.

One bright afternoon when the gods were playing their new game, Loki met Hod. "Why don't you join in the game?" Loki asked.

"How can you ask such a question? I'm blind," replied Hod.

"Still, you can throw a spear," Loki said.

"Why should I?" Hod asked, shrugging his shoulders.

"If you don't join them, the gods may think you don't like your brother," suggested Loki.

It was a clever argument. Hod and Balder were as different as two brothers could be. There was a rumor among the gods that Hod was jealous of Balder.

"All right," Hod agreed, "hand me a spear." Loki put the spear in Hod's hand and placed him opposite Balder.

The gods were pleased that Hod had agreed to join their game. They even cheered him on. It took time to show Hod just how to aim the spear at Balder's heart.

When Hod threw the spear, he drove it hard and straight. The gods looked on in horror as the spear found its mark. The prophecy had come true. Balder was dead — killed by his brother's hand.

When Odin learned what had happened, he sent a swift messenger to plead with Hela. Odin promised Hela any favor, if only he could have his son back.

Hela was a gloomy goddess and in no mood to give up Balder. But the request had come from Odin, highest of the gods. Hela said she would give Balder back to Odin on one condition. Everyone and everything, everywhere on earth, would have to weep for Balder.

The messenger returned to tell Odin of Hela's demands. And Odin sent out the word. Everyone and everything on earth was asked to weep for Balder. And it seemed they did. The women wept, the men wept. The animals and the trees and the birds wept. Tears dropped from every rose, from every flower and weed. Tears sprang from the rocks. The earth was bathed in tears.

The gods walked through the world and saw all this. Then they saw someone who didn't weep. It was an old woman sitting in front of a cave.

"You're not weeping," one of the gods said.

"Why should I?" the woman asked.

"Because Balder is dead," he told her.

"He meant nothing to me," she answered.
Before the god could argue with her, she disappeared into the cave.

They did not know the woman had been Loki in disguise. They were to learn that later. But because one creature had refused to weep, Hela would not give up Balder. So the gods prepared to send him to the world of the dead. He was placed on a ship with gifts from the gods. The casket was lit by a torch. Flames reached for the sky.

When the gods learned it had been Loki who refused to weep for Balder, they turned him out of Asgard.

But it was too late. The gods had been weakened by Loki's schemes and wicked advice. With Balder dead, they were no longer good enough or strong enough to govern the world. Loki went to Midgard. He caused even more mischief among the people there than he had among the gods. He took advantage of human weakness, human jealousy and greed. Under Loki's evil influence, brothers killed brothers, and fathers fought sons. Evil swept over the earth like a raging plague.

Odin was sad after Balder's death. But he grieved for the world when he learned of the dreadful state of things in Midgard. The ravens — Hugin, who was born of Odin's thoughts, and Munin, who served as his memory — flew out and came back with the shocking tales. Odin shook his head sadly. He could see that the end, the Twilight of the Gods, was not far off.

The Twilight of the Gods

Heimdall, keeper of the Gjallarhorn, was watchman for the gods. With Gjallarhorn, or "ringing horn," Heimdall could sound a warning heard in heaven, earth, and the underworld.

Heimdall lived at the entrance of the world, near the Rainbow Bridge that spanned Midgard and Asgard. He could see for hundreds of miles, and he could hear grass grow on the hills and wool grow on sheep. No one had sight or hearing as keen as Heimdall's. The gods, one day, would depend upon the sleepless sentry to summon them to the final battle with the giants. On that day, Heimdall's wonderful vision and hearing would alert him to the approach of the giants. Then he would sound a powerful blast on Gjallarhorn, warning the gods to prepare for the Great Battle. As the gods reckoned time, the fateful day was not far off.

The first warning that the end was near began with a three-year blizzard. Howling winds swept over the earth from the four points of the compass. The winds and snow clashed and whirled through winter, spring, summer, and fall.

There was another warning, closer to Asgard. The golden-combed rooster of the gods crowed shrilly and was answered by the rooster of Jotunheim and by the dark red rooster of Hel.

One dismal, icy dawn, Heimdall heard the winter winds
and the golden-combed rooster. He leaped up, seized his
horn, and ran to the bridge. The watchful god saw the
giants and the monsters coming toward Rainbow Bridge
from several directions. Heimdall raised his horn, took
a deep breath, and blew a terrible blast that was heard
around the world.

Odin had been expecting Heimdall's alarm. He sprang
up, put on the brightest of his battle clothes, and went

to his sons, Thor and Vidar. Odin found Thor lacing Vidar's shoe.

Vidar had a special destiny with that shoe. For years the shoemakers of Midgard had given Vidar the cuttings from all the shoes they made. Vidar had one enormous shoe made from these scraps. He would have need for the shoe on this final day of the gods. Today Vidar was wearing his heavy shoe for the first time, and Thor had his hammer fastened in his belt. Odin was proud of his valiant sons.

The All-father then went to round up the other gods. They all were ready, but were not as strong nor as well armed as they should have been. Odin's eye flashed when he saw Tyr, the god of war. He had only one hand. On this day, of all days, Tyr would need the hand that he had lost to the Fenris wolf.

When Odin saw Frey, his eye stared hard. Frey no longer had his famous sword. He had traded it for a bride, the daughter of a giant. Frey was clutching a stag's horn as a weapon. Yet there was no fear in Frey's eyes. He was prepared to stand firm against the enemy, ready to die the valiant death of the gods.

The same was true of the other gods. Odin had told them, "Though you may never stand in battle again, face the enemy and destroy him. When the battle is over, although the gods may themselves be destroyed, there will come another race of men to rule the world in peace." In a way, it was the most glorious day for the gods.

Heimdall was at the Rainbow Bridge watching the enemy approach. Loki led the massive column of giants

and monsters. There were gnarled dwarfs mounted on
swift horses, the shrieking hound of Hel, fearsome giants
towering over everything but the mountains, and most
fearful of all, the Fenris wolf, torn loose from his bonds
at last.

One of the gods would have to fight the Fenris wolf.
Thor vowed he would smash the monster with his hammer.
Odin said nothing. The god of wisdom knew that he was
destined to face the Fenris wolf and fulfill the prophecy.
The gods formed their blazoned battle lines and waited.

Skoll and Hati, the wolves that had been chasing the
sun and moon, were about to catch their prey. A giantess

had fed the wolves on the bones of murderers. There had been so many murdered people in Midgard that the wolves were well fed and had grown big and strong. Now they were determined to devour the sun and moon. In a final leap, the ravening wolves caught the sun and moon and swallowed them. A scream pierced the sky.

Instantly the sky went dark, the stars faded, the earth shook, and the mountains trembled with fear. The Midgard serpent pulled its many miles of body out of the sea, causing a tidal wave that flooded the earth.

The battle had begun. Thor rushed toward the Fenris wolf, whirling his powerful hammer. But the Midgard serpent, spitting his blinding, deadly poison, bound the god in his coils. Thor smashed his hammer at the slippery snake. Again and again he struck at the writhing, poisonous serpent.

Meanwhile, the snarling Fenris wolf leaped at Odin. The god thrust at him with his mighty spear. The wolf backed away howling, and sprang again. Odin had his spear ready to strike again. Before Odin's startled eye, the wolf grew and grew and grew. The wolf's wide-open, dripping jaws reached from the earth to the sky. He rushed at Odin and swallowed him whole.

But the Fenris wolf did not have long to gloat over his victory. Vidar, Odin's son, saw what had happened to his father and came running with his tremendous shoe, CLUMP——A-CLUMP, A-CLUMP.

The wolf turned on Vidar, with its huge mouth open, ready to swallow him. Vidar took a running jump and landed the heavy shoe on the wolf's lower jaw. He grabbed the upper jaw in his hands, and with a powerful wrench, tore the Fenris wolf apart. That was the end of Fenrir the wolf.

Thor was not far from Odin, but he could not see what had happened. He was blinded by the poison of the Midgard serpent. Thor gave the serpent a final blow with his mighty hammer. The Midgard serpent quivered and lay still.

Thor staggered nine steps. The poison of the Midgard serpent flooded Thor's veins, and the god fell dead.

As for Loki, the father of monsters and the evil genius of the gods, he was slain by Heimdall. They fought with such wild fury that they both fell dead. Most of the other giants and gods destroyed one another in the same mad frenzy.

Frey was the last god on the battlefield. He had been fighting a giant named Surt, who had a fiery sword. Frey fought fearlessly with the stag's horn. It took Surt a long time to kill Frey, but at last Surt killed him.

The giant, maddened by the long and bitter fight with the god, swung his fiery sword in all directions. Fire spurted from the sword and spread everywhere. The flames consumed everything in sight. Fire burned the earth until it was left a charred mass. Then it sank into the boiling sea. A few sparks hung over the black bubbles, flickered awhile, and faded. Then all was dark and still.

For a long time, a time that could not be measured since there no longer was night and day, there remained a vast gap of swirling shadows, the way it had been in the beginning. At last the earth slowly came out of the sea. A new sun, the daughter of the first sun, arose in the sky and warmed the earth. In a short time, a bright green spread over the land.

All evil had vanished in the flames of the Great Battle, and there came forth a far better life. The younger sons of Odin and Thor still lived in a lonely, glittering palace in Asgard. They were good and pure. For this reason, the Norse people say, they were spared.

Balder slept on in the mysterious realm of the dead. The god had slept through the roar of the battle. He had slept even through the long, dead silence, when there was neither day nor night. Now, with the awakening of a new life, Balder arose from the dead. He summoned his brother Hod from his grave, and they returned to Asgard. There they met the other young gods, and together they planned for a new world.

Deep in a forest a man and his wife, Lif and Lifthrasir, had been spared, too. They had slept a long time, waiting for the rebirth of life. Finally, they awoke and fed on the morning dew. Lif and Lifthrasir had a family. Their sons and daughters, and the children ever after them, brought forth on earth a new race of men.

Glossary

Asgard (AHS gahrd), the home of the gods

Ask (ahsk), the first man, made by the gods from an ash tree

Audhumbla (OWD hoom blah), a mythical cow. Audhumbla nursed the first giant, and by licking the salty ice, brought the first god into being.

Balder (BAWL dur), the god of light; a son of Odin and Frigga. He was slain by his brother Hod.

Bergilmir (bur GEL mir), the giant who escaped the deluge after Ymir's death and then established a new race of giants in Jotunheim

Brock (brok), the dwarf who won a bet with Loki

Elli (EL ee), a nurse to Utgard-loki's children; she represented old age.

Embla (EM blah), the first woman, made by the gods from an elm tree

Fenrir (FEN rir), the monster-son of Loki who had the form of a wolf

Frey (fray), the god of sunshine, rain, and harvest

Freya (FRAY uh), the goddess of love, beauty, and spring

Frigga (FRIG uh), the guardian of marriage; the wife of Odin

Gerda (GUR duh), daughter of the giant Gymir, and the wife of Frey

Gjallarhorn (YAHL lahr hawrn), "ringing horn"; Heimdall's horn, which sounded a warning to the gods on the day of the Great Battle

Heimdall (HAYM dahl), the watchman of the gods; the guardian of the Rainbow Bridge

Hela (HEL ah), a daughter of Loki who ruled the kingdom of the dead

Hod (hawd), the god of darkness; brother of Balder

Hugi (HYOO gee), thought, in the person of a young man

Hugin and **Munin** (HYOO gin; MOO nin), the two ravens of Odin. They brought him news of the whole world.

Idun (EE doon), the goddess who guarded the basket of golden apples

Jotunheim (YAW tun haym), the home of the giants

Lif and **Lifthrasir** (lif; LIF thrah sir), the man and woman who survived the Great Battle

Logi (LOH gee), Utgard-loki's cook who represented fire

Loki (LOH kee), the god of strife and the spirit of evil. He was at first accepted by the gods but later became their enemy.

Midgard (MID gahrd), "middle garden"; the country of man, created by the gods from Ymir's corpse

Midgard serpent (MID gahrd SUR punt), the serpent-son of Loki who wrapped himself around the world and held his tail in his mouth

Odin (OH din), the chief of the gods and a master of magic. He was the god of wisdom and poetry, of battle and the slain, and he inspired the gods to fierce heroism. According to legend, Odin traded his right eye for all the wisdom of the world.

Sif (sif), Thor's wife, whose golden hair was shorn by Loki

Sindri (SIN dree), the ruler of the dwarfs. He made the magic hammer for Thor, the golden boar for Frey, and the magic ring for Odin.

Skirnir (SKEER nir), a servant who helped Frey win the love of the giantess Gerda

Skoll and **Hati** (skul; HAH tee), the fierce wolves who chased, and later swallowed, the sun and the moon

Skrymir (SKREE mir), the name used by Utgard-loki when he first met Thor, Loki, and Thialfi on their way to Jotunheim

Surt (surt), the giant who destroyed the world by fire during the Great Battle

Thialfi (THYAHL vee), son of a Midgard farmer; the swiftest of all men

Thjazi (THYAHT see), the storm giant who stole Idun and the golden apples

Thor (thawr), the god of thunder; eldest son of Odin

Tyr (teer), the god of war, whose hand was bitten off by Fenrir

Utgard (OOT gahrd), a city in Jotunheim

Utgard-loki (OOT gahrd-LOH kee), the evil giant-king of Utgard

Vidar (VEE dahr), the god of justice; son of Odin. He killed Fenrir on the day of the Great Battle.

Ymir (EE mir), the first giant